Just Write!

Just Write!

Strategies To Build Writing Skill and Confidence

By Greta and Ted Rasmussen

ISBN 0-936110-22-8
Library of Congress Catalog Card Number: 99-71092
Copyright © 1999 by Greta Rasmussen
All rights reserved. Printed in the U.S.A.

TIN MAN PRESS
BOX 219
STANWOOD, WA 98292
www.tinmanpress.com

Contents

Introduction

This is a book that encourages children to write just for the fun of it. In the process, it is our hope that they will become more skillful writers, and will approach writing with less dread and more confidence.

"Just Write!" consists of 50 reproducible activity pages that focus on familiar subjects. You'll find topics such as "The My Page," "The Spill Page," "The Backwards Page," "The Worry Page," and "The Air Page." Since every page has a different theme, the writing projects are varied and unexpected. The fact that students can be counted on to know at least something about the individual topics provides the "hook" for getting them to communicate their ideas. Ask them about their thumbs ("The Hand Page"), or the biggest crowd they've ever been in ("The Crowded Page"), or the workings of a drawer ("The Furniture Page"), and you're bound to get some interesting results because they know a little about all of these things.

You will notice that each writing page is accompanied by a teacher page, which provides additional comments about the activities as well as possible responses. In many cases, there are really no right or wrong answers. Be prepared to accept anything a child can justify.

Also on the teacher page, we have included an extending activity to go along with each theme page. In every case, the extender focuses on a simple art challenge that relates to the general theme of the activity. Not only should these extenders help keep "early finishers" busy, they will also serve as fun-to-do rewards once the writing work is completed. If you choose to use the art ideas, you'll find they are very easy to administer. Most require only pencil and paper.

Of course, it is important to remind youngsters that you want them to treat these assignments with respect and that you expect them to put forth their best efforts. As you know, any activity can be raced through and, therefore, rendered meaningless. It should also be stressed that every part of the assignment must be completed.

Occasionally, some students may need more space than we have allotted for the various challenges. If that is so, simply tell them to finish their writing on the back of their activity sheets.

We hope you enjoy these activities and that "Just Write!" will be just right for your students.

Greta and Ted Rasmussen

The Happy Page

Possible Responses:

1.

2. A desk can't be happy because it isn't alive and can't think.

3. I can tell a dog is happy when it wags its tail and shakes all over. It also opens its mouth and looks like it is smiling.

4. Yes, I can be happy even when I'm doing something boring if I try to do it the best I can. (Or if I think about something that is interesting.)

5.

Comment:

We may have started something. Number 2 may evoke some spirited philosophical speculation.

Extender:

Have students draw that happy dog or cat they've described in Number 3.

Name_____

THE HAPPY PAGE

I can't smile.

1. Think about something you have done recently that has made someone happy. Write about it.

_____

_____

_____

_____

2. Why can't a desk be happy? _____

_____

3. DOGS & CATS

Pick either a dog or a cat and write about all the ways you can tell when it is happy.

I can tell a _____ is happy

when _____

_____

_____

_____

_____

_____

4. Can you be happy while you are doing a dull job? Write your opinion.

_____

_____

_____

_____

5. Fill up this smile with the names of famous people you'd be happy to know.

The Middle Page

Possible Responses:

1. I have a nose on my face.
   We don't get mail today because it is Sunday.
   If you'll go with me, I'll do it.
   The alarm sounded so loud I woke up.
   Things that go up always come down.

2. Each daisy has a brown spot in the middle.
   The path goes through the middle of the forest.

3. I was talking on the telephone when I heard a knock at the door.
   I hope that I can take the test early.

4. The circle is in the center of a square, and both are in a bigger square.

Comment:

Don't let students get by with lazy approaches to Number 1. Emphasize that responses such as "My nose runs" or "I go crazy" aren't good enough.

Extender:

Tell youngsters to draw a landscape, but here's the catch: The most interesting part of the picture should be located in the middle of their drawings.

Name_____

THE MIDDLE PAGE

1. Build sentences around these "middle" words.

_____ nose _____

_____ today _____

_____ go _____

_____ sounded _____

_____ up _____

2. Write two sentences about nature that include the word "middle."

_____

_____

_____

_____

Not me!

3. Someone cut these sentences in the middle. Finish the word and then finish each sentence any way you like.

I was talking on the tel_____

_____

I hope that I c_____

_____

4. Write a sentence describing this picture but don't use the word "middle."

_____

_____

_____

_____

The Answer Page

Possible Responses:

1. My name is Angela Baker.
   I am a girl living in the United States.
   I am a member of a family of six people.

2. Mud is dirt that has become wet and sticky.

3. A stick is a little branch that has fallen off a tree.

4. No.

   I'm sorry, but I've already made plans to go with Sally.

   Well, I don't know. I'll have to see. Maybe I might just see you out there.

   The mall? I went there just last Saturday and it was so busy. I had to stand in line forever to get a hamburger. And then I bought the cutest sweater. Do you want to see it?

Comment:

The fourth part of Number 4 will tell you something about the inventive abilities of your students.

Extender:

Give youngsters this challenge: Draw a picture of yourself with a puzzled look on your face because you don't know the answer.

THE ANSWER PAGE

Name_____

17698742?

1. Who are you? Give three different answers to this question. Use complete sentences.

_____

_____

_____

2. Answer this: "What is mud?"

_____

_____

_____

3. Answer this: "What is a stick?"

_____

_____

_____

4. Here is the question: "Can I go with you to the mall?"

Give the shortest answer you can. _____

Give a very polite answer that says "no." _____

_____

Give an answer that doesn't sound friendly. _____

_____

Give an answer that doesn't stay on the subject. _____

_____

_____

The Change Page

Possible Responses:

1.

2. You put meat or cheese between two slices of bread.

    You write a message on paper to someone.

    You wrap it up and give it to someone.

3. cart   animal
    fortune   begin

    I put some <u>animal</u> crackers into my grocery <u>cart</u>.

4. I am going bowling on Saturday.

Comment:

Encourage children to take some time with the first activity. To respond by saying, "John Doe, because he's rich, handsome, and cool," doesn't go far enough.

Extender:

Suggest to students that they illustrate the sentence they wrote in Number 3.

THE CHANGE PAGE

I'm going to change into an eagle!

1. Name a person you'd like to change places with for a day. Then explain why, including at least three reasons.

_____

_____

_____

_____

_____

2.

How do you change bread into a sandwich?

_____

_____

How do you change a piece of paper into a letter?

_____

_____

How do you change a book into a present?

_____

_____

3. Change the words below into longer words by adding letters to the end of each word. Then use two of your new words in a sentence.

car _____   an _____

for _____   be _____

_____

_____

_____

4. Change around the order of the words below to make a sentence, and then write it. You must use all the words.

am Saturday I bowling going on

_____

_____

The Pretend Page

Possible Responses:

1. How do you feel about not being able to go wherever you'd like to go?

   I'm not too upset about it now, but it was pretty hard at first because I used to roam free when I lived in Africa.

2. The first thing I heard when I woke up was a besquak coming from a tree.

   Besquak means birdsong.

   I slooked the water as fast as I could because I was thirsty.

   Slooked means drank.

3. There would be many problems, such as having a bed long enough, hitting my head on ceilings, buying clothes, and fitting into a car.

Comment:

You might share some of the sentences containing made-up words and let the class guess the meanings.

Extender:

Here's a drawing challenge for students: They are to pretend they've just seen a strange new animal that has two heads, a huge tail, and very weird-looking eyes. Let them take it from there.

THE PRETEND PAGE ~

1. Pretend you could have a real conversation with an elephant at the zoo. Write a question you might ask.

_____

_____

Now, write the answer you might receive.

_____

_____

2. Here's a made-up word: besquak. Pretend you know what it means and use it in an interesting sentence.

_____

_____

In the sentence I just made, besquak means:

_____

Write another sentence using a made-up word.

_____

_____

_____

In the sentence I just made, my word means:

_____

3. Pretend you are the tallest person in the world. What would some of your problems be?

_____

_____

_____

_____

_____

_____

The Straight Page

Possible Responses:

1. (See example on activity page.)

2.

3. Move the bottom right corner down a little bit.

4. Don't stop off and do anything else on the way home from school.

Comment:

Let's see what kind of ideas they generate for Number 2. Will anyone come up with pictures like these?

 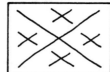 

Extender:

A straight-line picture is very much in order.

Name_____

THE STRAIGHT PAGE

1. Look at the two sentences on the right. They share a letter where the straight lines meet. Use the lines below to write two sentences that also share a letter where the lines meet.

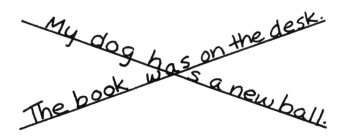

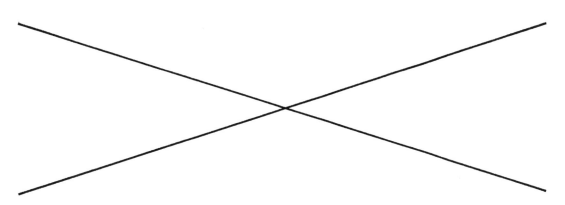

2. Each of the pictures below is made with 10 straight lines, and each has its own idea. Make your own 10-line picture in the blank box and then describe your idea.

_____

_____

_____

3.  If you had to give this person direc-tions about how to straighten the picture, what would you tell him?

_____

_____

_____

4. "I want you to come straight home after school." What does this mean? Write the sentence in another way.

_____

_____

_____

The Same Page

Possible Responses:

1. We were almost out of milk so I went to the grocery store and bought more.

2. By having the number the same, almost all people will know it, no matter where they are.

3. Same faces,
   Same hairdos,
   Same clothes,
   But inside,
   They're different.

4.

5. These faces look the same except they're facing a different way.

Comment:

About Number 4: If any of your students don't watch TV, have them write about a favorite radio program, or magazine, or even a piece of music.

Extender:

Draw a design on the board and ask students to repeat the same design on their papers. Try something like this:

THE SAME SAME SAME PAGE

1. Write this sentence in a different way but keep the same meaning:

I realized we didn't have much milk in the house,
so I had to go out and buy some.

_____

_____

2.  Why is the emergency telephone number 911 the same all across the country?

_____

_____

3. Make up a poem about twins. Use the word "same" as many times as you can.

4. You probably watch some of the same programs on TV week after week. Name one of your favorite shows and tell why you like it.

_____

_____

_____

_____

_____

5. Describe this picture, using the word "same" any way you wish.

_____

_____

The Talk Page

Possible Responses:

1.

2. Person 1 – Because I enjoy it.

    Person 2 – Because it gives me something to do and anyway, I'm a big sports fan, so I always catch the Tigers whenever I can. Did you know they're going to be on TV again this Friday?

3. I chose the top one because the line looks uneven, like talking. The other line looks smooth, like singing.

4. On Wednesday I came to school but didn't feel well and had to go home early.

Comment:

Other answers for Number 4 might be: I lost my voice and could hardly speak, or I only knew one of the answers so I didn't talk much.

Extender:

Ask students to draw a couple of cartoon characters with bubbles above their heads. What are they talking about? How about the weather – or something you've discussed in class recently?

Name_____

THE TALK PAGE

1. Who do you most enjoy talking with? Why? _____

_____

_____

_____

2. Two people are asked the same question, "Why do you watch TV?" Person 1 doesn't like to talk much. Person 2 likes to talk a lot. Tell how you think these people would answer the question.

Person 1 _____

Person 2 _____

_____

_____

_____

3. One of these people is talking. One is singing. Put a check mark by the person you think is talking and explain your answer.

_____

_____

4. Here is how much you talked in school on Monday, Tuesday, Thursday, and Friday: ☐☐☐☐

Here is how much you talked on Wednesday: ▫

What could have been going on with you on Wednesday?

_____

_____

_____

The Baby Page

Possible Responses:

1. Very tiny babies can't walk or stand up or read or say real words.

2. It means that the person is acting spoiled or younger than he or she really is.

3. Tweet lil baby, time to wash your ittle handies and footsies and then mama will get you some milkie.

4. Drawing B was most likely made by a baby because it's just a scribble. Babies can't control the marks they make.

Comment:

About Number 4: We all know that a two-week-old baby couldn't hold a pencil, much less make a scribble. So we're talking about older babies here.

Extender:

Have children pretend they are babies and scribble on a piece of drawing paper. Then, have them go back to their "real age" and find shapes in the scribbles that can be turned into real things – flowers, fanciful animals, cartoon people, etc.

THE BABY PAGE

1. Use all the blanks to write about some things that babies can't do.

Very tiny babies can't _____

_____

_____

_____

2. If someone is acting like a baby, what does that mean?

_____

_____

_____

_____

3. Use some of these baby-talk words (or any others you wish) to write a few things a mom might say to her baby.

footsies	goo goo	tummy	dada	boo-boo	mama	milkie
ittle	handies	wet wet	cutie pie	tweetie	umm-umm	

_____

_____

_____

_____

_____

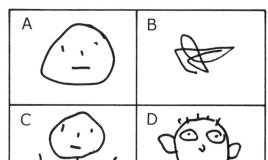

4. Which of these drawings was most likely made by a baby? How can you tell?

_____

_____

_____

_____

The Tooth Page

Possible Responses:

1. It was very hard to pronounce the words, and they didn't come out clearly at all.

2. I have a loose tooth.

3. This is a
   brush
   in a
   rush!

4. An elbow is something like a knee, and a finger is something like a toe, but a tooth isn't like any other part of your body.

5.

Comment:

You might consider taking a poll to find out how many students have loose teeth right now.

Extender:

Ask children to draw a picture of themselves brushing their teeth. This may be hard for them to do, but see how they handle it.

 THE TOOTH PAGE ~

 I'm brushing my beak!

1. Put your tongue on your front teeth and try to say this sentence: "Louis looked to the left." What happened?

_____

_____

_____

_____

2. "I have a lse tth."

Add four o's and write this sentence the way it really should be written.

_____

_____

3. FINISH THIS RHYME.

This is a

brush

in a

_____ !

 I'm late!

4. FINISH THIS SENTENCE.

An elbow is something like a knee, and a finger is something like a toe, but a tooth . . .

_____

_____

5. Tell the whole story about losing your first tooth. Include where and when it came out, and how you felt when it happened.

_____

_____

_____

_____

_____

The Sports Page

Possible Responses:

1.

2. A basketball has just hit the rim of the basket but didn't go in.

   One player kicked the soccer ball and another player jumped up to block it.

   The ball bounced through the second baseman's legs.

3. They wouldn't be good names for sports teams because they don't sound tough enough.

4. Yes, that happens. Some people have great physical skills but might not have learned how to think of other people's feelings.

Comment:

Try to encourage youngsters to think carefully about their answer for Number 1 and to go beyond obvious first responses, such as: "He's a really good player."

Extender:

Say to students: Draw a picture of you playing your favorite sport. Put yourself in a cool uniform, if you wish.

THE SP⚾RTS PAGE ~

Anyone seen my glove?

1. Who is your favorite sports star? Why?

_____

_____

_____

2. Write a complete sentence about what's going on in each of these pictures.

_____

_____

_____

_____

_____

_____

3. Lots of sports teams have names like the Tigers or Bulldogs. Why don't you ever hear about teams called the Mice or the Chipmunks?

_____

_____

_____

_____

4. Can a person be a good player but not be a good sport? Explain.

_____

_____

_____

_____

_____

The Slow Page

Possible Responses:

1. Circle A is a little wiggly, but it is rounder-looking. Circle B is sloppy.

2. I can't say for sure because I don't know if they started at the same time.

3. Because these are two slow things. But to the caterpillar, the turtle seems fast.

4. Swallowing.

5. Things seem to go most slowly when I'm doing something I don't want to do.

   It's best to go slowly when you're doing homework.

Comment:

If one of your students answers Number 2 this way, "Maybe the bottles didn't have the same amount of soda pop in them to start with," keep your eye on that youngster – you have an interesting intellect on your hands.

Extender:

Bring in a leaf or stick or pretzel for each student. Then instruct them to draw the object as slowly and carefully as they can.

THE PAGE

Good!
A slow bug!

1. Draw a circle as slowly as you can in Box A. Then draw a circle as quickly as you can in Box B.

How are your two circles different? Look carefully and describe what you see.

A

B

_____

_____

_____

_____

2. Can you say for sure that the person on the right is drinking more slowly? Why or why not?

_____

_____

_____

3. This cartoon isn't really funny, but it's a little funny. Why?

Hey!
Slow down

_____

_____

_____

4. Which is slower, blinking or swallowing?

_____

5. FINISH THESE SENTENCES.

Things seem to go most slowly when

_____

_____

It's best to go slowly when _____

_____

_____

The Circle Page

Possible Responses:

1. "Hey, I have an idea! If you turn around, we could get together and make a circle."

2.

3. All the action words (verbs) are trying to get out of the circle.

4. When people are arranged in a circle, everyone can see and hear everyone else more easily.

Comment:

Number 3 provides excellent practice in analytical thinking. It may take students a while to figure out what is happening, but that's okay. And if a less analytical child says "some of the words are trying to get out," that's good enough.

Extender:

Tell students that you want them to make a design using 50 circles. The circles can be big, small, dark, spotted, whatever. They can also touch each other or overlap. But you want an interesting design!

I prefer ovals!

1. FINISH THE SENTENCE.

"Hey, I have an idea! If you turn around, we could get together and . . .

_____ ."

2. What have you done in school today so far? There is a short sentence already written around the smallest circle shown below. Write two more sentences around the other circles.

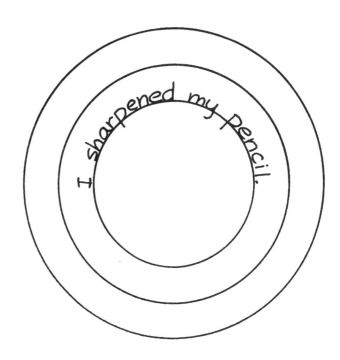

I sharpened my pencil.

3. Look at the picture and then describe what might be going on. Hint: Read the words carefully. There's a pattern!

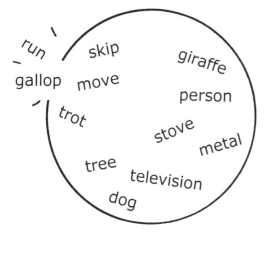

run
skip
giraffe
gallop move
person
trot
stove
metal
tree
television
dog

_____

_____

_____

4. Why is it better to have people sit in a circle rather than at a long table when they are discussing something?

_____

_____

_____

_____

_____

The Brain Page

Possible Responses:

1. I thought about what I was going to wear to school.
    I wondered if it would rain.
    I hoped my mom made me a good lunch.
    I thought about a book I read last night.
    I remembered that I needed to bring my homework to school.

2. bounce – ball, round, Earth, spaceship, astronaut, job, work
    blue – sky, air, lungs, body, person, talk, phone

3. I have a dull point on my pencil and it should be sharper. I need to pick up my pencil. I need to know what the pencil sharpener looks like and where it is located. I need to place the pencil into the sharpener hole and turn the handle. I need to know when it's time to take out the pencil.

Comment:

There are many thoughts that can be expressed in Number 3, since the brain has to process so much information even for the simplest act. You might want to take a few extra minutes and talk about all the possible ways to answer this question. Or ask students to think of all the processes the brain goes through when a person puts on socks!

Extender:

Cover up the pencil sharpener in your room with a bag or piece of paper, and ask students to draw it from memory.

Name_____

THE (BRAIN) PAGE ~

I have a bird brain!

1. Write several sentences about things you've thought about today. Start each sentence with the word "I," and make all of your sentences interesting.

_____

_____

_____

_____

_____

_____

2. BRAINSTORMS

Do some brainstorming! Each word must have something to do with the word that goes above it. Look at the example first.

cat	bounce	blue
fur	_____	_____
soft	_____	_____
pillow	_____	_____
sleep	_____	_____
bed	_____	_____
sheet	_____	_____
cloth		

3. Think about it! What are some of the things your brain needs to tell you when you use a pencil sharpener?

_____

_____

_____

_____

_____

_____

_____

_____

The Birthday Page

Possible Responses:

1. A birthday takes note of the day, month, and year you were born.

2. I am planning a surprise birthday party for Sylvia Ramirez. Please come to my house at 1012 Main Street at 4 p.m. on Friday, June 12. Please bring a present that doesn't cost too much money.

3. It is a sunny day. A birthday party is taking place. Six kids are sitting at the table and the girl who is having the birthday is just about ready to blow out her candles. She is seven years old today. Her dad is taking a picture. Her mother is holding her baby sister, and her big sister is holding a present. A dog and cat are there, too, and a bird is watching from a branch.

Comment:

Number 1 is harder to answer than you might imagine, because the meaning of the word includes the commemoration of the event as well as the event itself. (We suspect students won't say this in quite the same manner.)

Extender:

Have youngsters draw a picture of their dream birthday cake in honor of their upcoming birthday, and see if they add an extra candle to indicate their new age.

1. What is a birthday? _____

_____

2. You are planning a surprise birthday party for your friend. Write an invitation to the people you're going to invite. Tell them everything they will need to know about coming to your party.

_____

_____

_____

_____

3. This is a picture of somebody's birthday party. Use the blanks to tell as much about the picture as you can. If you need more space, use the back of your paper.

_____

_____

_____

_____

_____

_____

The Spill Page

Possible Responses:

1.

2. The "B" bowl is flatter on the bottom, so it would be harder to tip over.

3. Dear Aunt Jane,
   I'm sorry that
   we couldn't go
   to the concert.
   I hope we can
   go another time.

   Love,
     Jenny

4. Because things that spill usually spread out unevenly.

Comment:

Number 4 might be difficult because what is so obvious is sometimes hard to put into words. Children can hardly be expected to say that the edges of the spill will have an irregular configuration due to the random nature of the dynamics of liquid dispersion.

Extender:

Continuing the thinking youngsters did for Number 2, ask them to design a fancy glass that might tip over easily, and a practical glass that would be less likely to tip.

Name_____

oops!

1. Describe a time you spilled something and really made a mess.

_____
_____
_____
_____

2. A dog eating from dish "B" would be less likely to spill its food than a dog eating from dish "A." Why?

A   B

_____
_____
_____

3.

SPLAT!

Someone spilled on this letter. Use the space below to write the whole letter again.

Dear Aunt Jane,
I'm sorry that
we couldn't go
to the
I hop
go
Lov
Jenn

_____
_____
_____
_____
_____
_____
_____

4. "A" looks more like a spill than "B." Explain why.

_____
_____
_____

The Old Page

Possible Responses:

1.

2. It gets brown spots on it.
   It grows very large.
   It looks out of style.
   It gets wrinkled and soft.

3. A bird doesn't live as long and so it will get old in a shorter period of time than a person.

4. There wouldn't be enough space for 50 candles, so each of the five big candles stands for 10 years.

Comment:

Some children may have difficulty with the concept expressed in the third activity. Point out that many birds live just three or four years and, therefore, it can be said that they are old by the time they reach the age of three. It also might be fun to ask why a bird doesn't look old. (Even if they did get wrinkles, it would be hard to see them under all those feathers, wouldn't it? And it would also be a struggle to fit them with glasses!)

Extender:

Instruct students to crumple up a piece of paper so it has a lot of wrinkles. Then have them smooth it out and draw an old person's face.

THE OLD PAGE

oh, no!
A gray feather!

1. Who is the oldest person you know? Tell as much as you can about that person, and be sure to include a good description of how he or she looks.

_____

_____

_____

_____

_____

_____

2. What do these things look like when they get old?

A banana _____

A tree _____

A car _____

A dollar bill _____

3. A bird gets old faster than a person. Why?

_____

_____

_____

_____

_____

4. Here is a birthday cake for someone who is 50 years old. Why do you think there are only five candles?

_____

_____

_____

_____

The I Can Page

Possible Responses:

1. I can always say the alphabet correctly.

    I can usually hit a baseball somewhere.

    I can almost make a cake by myself.

    I can never be in second grade again.

    When I try hard, I can read a newspaper.

2.

3. Dear Young,

    We saw these mountains
    yesterday, and tonight
    we are sleeping in a
    tent. So far, I have
    seen two deer.

    Carolyn

Comment:

Number 2 may give you some interesting insights into the way your students perceive themselves.

Extender:

Ask children to draw the other side of the postcard, making a picture of what they have just described.

Name_____

THE I CAN PAGE

So can I!

1. I CAN finish these sentences!

I can always _____

_____

I can usually _____

_____

I can almost _____

_____

I can never _____

_____

When I try hard, I can _____

_____

2. Think of something you have learned to do really well and write about it. Try to make your description so interesting that someone else might like to try it.

_____

_____

_____

_____

_____

_____

_____

3. I CAN write a postcard!

You're on a vacation and you've bought a postcard of something you have seen. Tell your best friend about it.

TO:

The Shadow Page

Possible Responses:

1. Because you have to have light in order to make shadows.

2. One day, Rover begged to go outside. The sun was out, and he felt very happy as he trotted out into the middle of the yard. Then, he saw a big dark shape that frightened him. It seemed to be following him! He started running very fast, but it stayed right behind him until he dived under the back porch. Then, that dark thing went away!

3. moose, deer, or chicken.
   bird or butterfly.
   space alien's head or turtle's head.

4.

Comment:

About Number 4: If students don't know how to "shadow" a letter, have them look at the word "shadow" in the title.

Extender:

Have children illustrate the dog stories they wrote for Number 2.

THE SHADOW PAGE

Hi !

1. You wouldn't find a shadow in a completely dark room. Why not?

_____

2. Write a story about a dog that is afraid of its own shadow.

_____

_____

_____

_____

_____

_____

_____

3. Here are three "hand shadows" someone has made on a wall. What do you think they could be?

 _____

 _____

 _____

4. Write the first letter of your first name in the box and shadow it. Then use that letter as the beginning of the first word in a sentence that tells something about yourself.

The Missing Page

Possible Responses:

1. There were triangles all over the place. Some of them were dangling from ropes in the sky. Some of them were pretending to be part of a salad. Some of them were hiding behind rocks. Some of them were using their points to pop balloons. And do you know what? They were having just a wonderful time!

2. Smdy, ll cts wll hv t wr cllrs.
   Somday, al cat wil hav t war colars.

3. I sing very well.
   Is it time to go?
   Sing me a song.
   In time, I'll be an adult.

4. A boy missing a tooth is looking at a clock missing a hand.

Comment:

About Number 3: You may have to remind students that all cross-outs take place in the word "missing."

Extender:

Instruct children to illustrate the crazy triangle story they completed in Number 1.

Name_____

THE _____ PAGE _ _ _ MISSING   I found it!

1. Fill in the missing parts of this wacky story any way you wish. (You must add several words to each sentence – see the example.)

There were triangles all over the place.

Some of them **were dangling from ropes** in the sky.

Some of them _____ salad.

Some of them _____ rocks.

Some of them _____ balloons.

And do you know what? They were having just a wonderful time!

2. Read this sentence: Someday, all cats will have to wear collars.
Rewrite it below – with all of the vowels missing.

_____

Now, rewrite the original sentence again, this time with one letter missing from each word. Try to take out the least important letters.

_____

3. Cross out some of the letters from the word "missing" to form sentences that make sense.

For example:
~~missing~~ your test finished?

missing very well.

missing it time to go?

missing me a song.

missing time, I'll be an adult.

4. Write a sentence about this picture. Use the word "missing" two times.

_____

_____

_____

The How Page

Possible Responses:

1. How long does it take to milk a cow?

2. How did the movie end?

3. It doesn't matter how you dress today.

4. Scissors have two sharp blades that come together to make a cut.

5. When will we get to where we're going?

6. You drop the marble into Funnel A and then it goes through a spiral into Funnel B and into a box and through a tube and into the dish.

Comment:

Another possible answer for Number 5 would be "When will we arrive?"

Extender:

Tell students to draw their own marble machines. Then think about constructing one as a class project. Collect a lot of paper towel tubes, get a roll of masking tape, some heavy paper, and go for it!

THE HOW PAGE

Name_____

I know how to fly!

49

1. Use the word "how" in a question about cows.

_____

2. Use the word "how" in a question about a movie.

_____

3. Now, finish this "how" sentence:

_____ matter how _____

4. How do scissors work? Write a simple explanation.

_____

_____

_____

_____

5. "How long until we get there?" Write a sentence that means about the same thing without using the words "how" or "there."

_____

_____

_____

_____

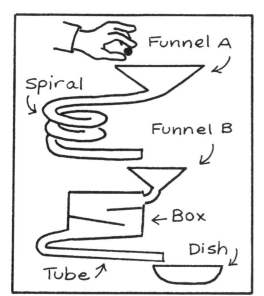

6. Pretend the "marble machine" on the left is made of clear plastic and that you are looking at it from the side. Describe how the marble will get down to the dish.

_____

_____

_____

_____

_____

The Eye Page

Possible Responses:

1. Blink means to close and open both eyes very quickly.

   Stare means to look in the same place for a very long time.

   Glance means to look at something for a very short time.

   Wink means to close one eye and then open it.

   Peek means to look at something without letting anyone else know you're doing it.

2. Wall, window, picture, map, floor, pencil sharpener, ceiling, light, chalk, eraser, wastebasket, paper, pencil, shirt, button, shelf, book, bulletin board, push pin, photograph, etc.

3. I'll watch your dog for you.

   The video made me understand why bike helmets are important.

Comment:

The intention in Number 2 is to encourage observation and fluency. If children write five words and then look up blankly, remind them that they're holding a <u>pencil</u>, and that their <u>desks</u> are resting on the <u>floor</u>.

Extender:

All the animals on a strange planet have developed big eyes because they spend most of their time in the dark. What would they look like? Have students draw several of them.

THE  EYE PAGE ~

Eye
see
seeds!

1. Here are some things you can do with your eyes. Describe what each word means.

blink _____

_____

stare _____

_____

glance _____

_____

wink _____

_____

peek _____

_____

3. Below are two sentences that include sayings about eyes. Write them in a different way without changing the meaning.

I'll keep an eye on your dog for you.

_____

_____

That video really opened my eyes about the need for bike helmets.

_____

_____

2. WHAT DO YOU SEE?

From where you are sitting, you can see dozens and dozens of things! Make a list and don't stop until you've run out of room. One rule: no people, just things!

_____

_____

_____

_____

_____

_____

_____

_____

_____

_____

_____

_____

_____

The Rules Page

Possible Responses:

1. Always be nice to each other.

2. I don't have to get permission to go to the bathroom. I don't have to line up to eat lunch. I don't have to raise my hand before speaking.

3. If the person who is IT touches you, then you become IT.

4. Jump twice when you see a robin.
   Always wear red when you go into stores.
   Never put chickens on your head.

Comment:

It should be interesting to find out how your students think about the issue raised in Number 1. Will they all basically follow the same idea or will you get a variety of opinions?

Extender:

Ask students to draw a picture of someone following one of their silly rules.

Name_____

THE RULES PAGE

1. Write one rule you think people should follow all of the time.

_____

_____

2. What is one school rule you don't need to follow at home?

_____

_____

_____

_____

3. What is the most important rule in the game of tag?

_____

_____

_____

_____

4. Let's write some really silly rules! In the frames on the right, you'll find two rules that don't make any sense. Write three of your own in the frames below.

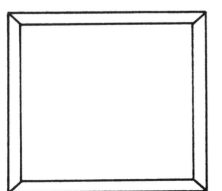

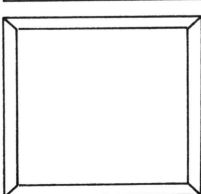

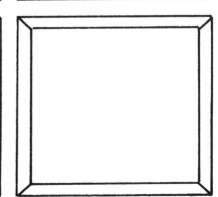

The Noise Page

Possible Responses:

1. I was fast asleep when I was suddenly awakened by scratching noises. Then I saw a big shape that looked like a giant toe. It was coming toward me! I started screaming. Then I woke up and looked at my feet. All my toes were there.

2. crunch - cracker; snap – rubber band; roar – lion; splat - egg dropping; splash - diver; hum - refrigerator running; pop - bubble bursting; squeak - chair; rumble - thunder; rattle - car

3. A. Hiccups
   B. Motor running
   C. Someone talking, shouting, and then talking again

Comment:

In Number 1, "toe" has been inserted into the story mix as a surprise element. You should get some interesting plot lines as a result.

Extender:

Direct students to illustrate their scary story. If a vampire bat is biting a toe, that would be a good visual.

 THE NOISE PAGE

1. Finish this story in the scariest way you can. But here's the catch: You must use some form of the words "noise," "scream," and "toe" somewhere in your story.

I was fast asleep when _____

_____

_____

_____

2. Do some brainstorming about noise! Name one thing that could make these noises. One rule: All of your answers have to be different.

crunch _____

snap _____

roar _____

splat _____

splash _____

hum _____

pop _____

squeak _____

rumble _____

rattle _____

3. Pretend each of the lines below stands for sounds you can hear. Tell what each of the sounds could be.

A	⋎⋎ ⋎⋎ ⋎⋎ ⋎⋎
B	～～～～～～
C	⋀⋀⋀⋀⋀～～

Line A _____

_____

Line B _____

_____

Line C _____

_____

The Question Page

Possible Responses:

1. What did you have for dessert?
    Do you want to go camping?
    When will your mother get back from her trip?
    Why didn't you bring the other suitcase?
    Why didn't you play the game?
    Do you want to go to the store?
    Who is the oldest person in your family?
    Why don't you ever eat hamburgers?

2. Who is the fastest runner in our class?
    Why did you turn off the television?
    Which one had the best score on the test?
    When was the last time you ate pizza?

3.

4. Why are you upside down?

Comment:

If, in Number 3, students ask the ultimate question, "Why am I doing this?" tell them it's good for them.

Extender:

Challenge students with this little scenario: Several question-mark people are playing a game against some exclamation-point people. Draw them playing, and don't forget their faces, of course.

 THE QUESTION PAGE

Name_____

Which way is south?

1. Here are some answers. You write the questions.

Three cookies. _____

I really do! _____

Maybe tomorrow. _____

It was too heavy. _____

It rained. _____

I can't. _____

My grandmother. _____

I can't stand them. _____

 2. Finish these questions any way you wish. Don't forget the question mark.

Who is _____

_____

Why did _____

_____

Which one had _____

_____

When was _____

_____

3. Write your teacher a question inside this question mark.

4. What question is Person A probably asking Person B?

A   B

_____

_____

The Money Page

Possible Responses:

1. If you'll give me a dime,
    I'll tell you the time.

    If you'll give me some money,
    I'll say something funny.

    I cost just a nickel
    'cause I'm just a pickle.

    I'm a dollar bill
    and I'm walking up a hill.

2. Dogs don't need money because everything they need is bought for them by people.

3.

4. A stick you find in your yard isn't worth any money because there are so many of them, and anybody can find them.

Comment:

In Number 1, you may need to tell students that the ending word in the second line should rhyme with the ending word in the first line. Also, the second line should make sense with the picture.

Extender:

Ask children to draw a picture of something that costs lots of money.

Name_____

THE  PAGE ~

what's money?

1. Look at the pictures and finish the rhymes.

 If you'll give me a dime,

I'll _____

 If you'll give me some money,

I'll _____

 I cost just a nickel

'cause I'm _____

 I'm a dollar bill

and I'm _____

2. FINISH THIS SENTENCE.

 Dogs don't need money because . . .

_____

_____

_____

_____

_____

_____

_____

3. If I suddenly had lots of money, I would _____

_____

_____

_____

_____

4. A stick you find in your yard isn't worth any money because _____

_____

_____

The Dishes Page

Possible Responses:

1.

2. I'd choose a bowl, because it would hold both solid and liquid foods.

3. I could turn it into a turtle by adding four legs, a head, and a tail. I could also show the pattern of the shell.

4. He can tell you when you do something wrong but he doesn't like it when you criticize him.

Comment:

Other possibilities for Number 3: a rainbow (by adding several arching lines); an ice-cream cone (by adding the cone part); a setting sun (by extending the base line); etc.

Extender:

Tell children to draw a big circle representing a dinner plate and then to decorate it with a pattern that pleases them.

THE DISHES PAGE ~

1. Describe everything you can about the dishes you have at home. What color are they? What decorations do they have on them? What do the various pieces look like?

_____

_____

_____

_____

2. If you had to eat from either a plate or a bowl for the rest of your life, which would you choose? Why?

_____

_____

_____

_____

4. "He can dish it out, but he can't take it." What do you think a saying like this might mean? If you don't know, take a guess.

_____

_____

_____

_____

3. The drawings below started out as upside-down bowls, but someone turned three of them into something else. What could you do to the fourth bowl to turn it into something else? Write about it <u>first</u>, then do it.

_____

_____

_____

_____

The Poem Page

Possible Responses:

1. Trees stand
   like giant
   soldiers guarding
   my yard.

                     A
                   tree
                 waves
               to me as
              the wind
             blows and
            rustles the
           green branches.

2. Back and forth,
   back and forth,
   the windshield
   wipers wipe.
   Back and forth,
   back and forth,
   they wipe the
   rain away.

3. I went too
   fast and had to
   pay the price for
   falling down today.
   It really hurt.

Comment:

Obviously, the quality of poetry will vary greatly, but this is a time to be accepting, as long as everyone tries. Many students will probably approach the first challenge with simple adjectives, such as: trees, green, rustling, pretty, etc. Though not very exciting, it'll do.

Extender:

Ask students to illustrate one of their poems.

 THE POEM PAGE ~

need
feed
seed

1. Guess what . . . these are poet-trees! So get ready to write some poet-tree (poetry). Read the instructions below before you start.

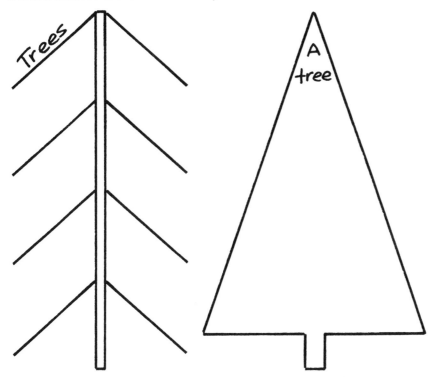

Trees

A tree

2. Write a poem you might say as you watch the windshield wipers of a car go back and forth.

A poem has started to grow at the top of each tree! On the left, finish the poem by writing words on each branch. On the right, fill up the tree with your poem. (None of the poems on this sheet needs to rhyme.)

3.

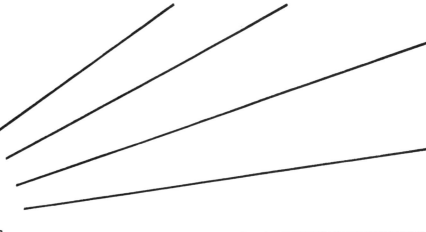

A FALLING DOWN POEM

Write a little poem about falling down. Put it on the falling-down lines.

The Backwards Page

Possible Responses:

1. People don't walk backwards very often because they would not be able to see where they were going. They would bump into things.

2.

3. First, I swallowed. Then, I chewed. Then, I put the food in my mouth. Then, I brought the fork to my mouth. Then, I picked up the food with my fork.

4. The fudge was so sticky that I had to go wash my hands.
   The fog was so thick that I couldn't see where I was going.
   The room was so small that there was space for just three people.

Comment:

Number 3 is hard. That's why we don't tell them how far back to go, or where the beginning is! Some students will be happy to do just one or two steps.

Extender:

Instruct children to write their complete name backwards. Suggest that they use big block letters so that the names can be decorated.

Name_____

EHT SDRAWKCAB EGAP
(THE BACKWARDS PAGE)

1. Walking backwards is really quite easy. Why don't people do it more often?

_____

_____

2. If you could see backwards, what would you be looking at right now?

_____

_____

_____

_____

3. THINK BACKWARDS.

"First, I went to sleep. Then, I went to bed. Next, I put on my pajamas." Get the picture? Now, finish this backwards story with lots of details.

First, I swallowed. Then, _____

_____

_____

_____

_____

4. These sentences start with words that are written backwards. Finish them with real words that make sense in the sentence.

Eht egduf saw os ykcits taht . . .

_____

_____

Eht gof saw os kciht taht . . .

_____

_____

Eht moor saw os llams taht . . .

_____

_____

The Wish Page

Possible Responses:

1. A wish is something you hope will happen.

2. I wish that I could paint nice pictures, spend a day at my friend's house, etc.

3. Wishes pop up in my head almost every day.
   I once wished for a bicycle but I never got it.
   Sometimes, wishes don't come true.
   Hyenas probably don't make wishes.

4. Mary wasn't sure she'd get her wish because she didn't blow out all the candles on her cake. But a friend helped her blow out the last candle and she got what she'd wished for anyway – a puppy.

Comment:

The writing assignment in Number 4 is more complicated than it might first seem. Not only must the idea of a wish be dealt with, but also the problem of the unextinguished candle must be addressed.

Extender:

Tell them to draw a picture of one of their sentences in Number 3.

Name_____

THE WISH PAGE

1. What is a wish? _____

_____

2. Describe some things you might wish for that don't cost money. _____

_____

_____

3. Below is the word "wish" written up and down. Use each letter as the beginning letter in the first word of a sentence that has something to do with making a wish.

W _____

_____

I _____

_____

S _____

_____

H _____

_____

4. This girl has a problem, but you can help her by making up a little story that has a happy ending. You should use some form of the word "wish" in your story.

_____

_____

_____

_____

_____

_____

The Hand Page

Possible Responses:

1. Gloves let you use your fingers so that you can do more things.

2. band, grand, sand, land, planned.

3. My thumb is attached to my hand in a different way. My thumb bends in just two places, not three places. My thumb is a lot thicker than my fingers.

4. I curl up my fingers as tightly as I can. Then I bend my thumb and put it against my fingers.

5. Don't crack your knuckles.
   Clip your fingernails.
   Go wash your hands.

Comment:

To emphasize the importance of thumbs, have students try to pick up a pencil and write with it without using their thumbs at any time.

Extender:

Ask children to make an interesting design by tracing around various parts of their hands. Suggest that they draw around their thumbs, and the V-shapes formed by their spread fingers, and their fists, etc.

1. Both mittens and gloves will keep your hands warm. Why is it sometimes better to wear gloves?

_____

_____

_____

_____

_____

2. Think of words starting with the letters below that rhyme with hand.

b _____

g _____

s _____

l _____

p _____

3. Write a short paragraph about how your thumbs are different from your fingers.

_____

_____

_____

_____

_____

4. How do you make a fist? Explain.

_____

_____

_____

_____

5. Your mother might say these things about hands. Fill in the blanks.

Don't crack your _____

Clip your _____

Go wash _____

The Hot Page

Possible Responses:

1. I am metal with one flat surface that smooths out cloth. A cord comes out of one end of me. What am I?

2. A Hot Dog Meets a Hot Dog on a Hot Day
    Help! The Letters Are Melting!

3. The Tigers are still on a hot streak. In a 76-58 romp over the Eagles last night, the Tigers chalked up their tenth win in a row.

Comment:

About Number 3: Here's your chance to talk about how colorful words contribute to good writing. Brainstorm various words that can take the place of "beat." Words such as "crushed," "overpowered," "bested," "pounded," and "smashed" beat "beat" every time, yes?

Extender:

Ask students to make a picture showing three different stages in the life of a snowman. Have them show the snowman as he looked when he was just made, as he is beginning to melt, and when he's almost melted away.

THE HOT PAGE

1. Write a riddle about something that gets hot. Two rules: You can't use its name when you describe it – or it wouldn't be a riddle. And you must give at least four clues about it (how it looks, what it does, etc.).

I am _____

_____

_____ What am I ?

2. Think of interesting titles for these two "hot" pictures.

_____   _____

_____   _____

3. If a sports team is on a winning streak, people often say it is "hot." Last night your basketball team, the Tigers, won its tenth game in a row. The score was 76-58. The team they played is called the Eagles.

Write the first paragraph of a newspaper story about this game. You <u>must</u> use the word "hot" and you <u>can't</u> use the word "beat."

_____

_____

_____

_____

The Shoe Page

Possible Responses:

1. I never wear shoes when I am taking a bath or when I go to bed or when I am swimming.

2. You can tell a shoe is old if it has a hole in the sole.
    All shoes are worn on the feet.
    Some shoes don't have laces.

3.

4. One is probably a woman wearing high heels. She seems to be shorter than the other person because she is taking smaller steps. The other person is probably a man wearing boots. He has a hole in his left boot.

Comment:

Encourage children to take a very close look at their shoes before they begin their written response for Number 3. Remind them that one of the keys to good writing is to know your subject. This entails close observation.

Extender:

First, have students draw around one of their shoes. Then, inside the outline, have them list every surface they've stepped on today.

Hi, left! Hi, right!

THE SHOE PAGE

Name_____

Don't need 'em!

1. Finish this sentence: I never wear shoes when _____

_____ or when _____

or when _____

2. FINISH THESE SENTENCES.

You can tell a shoe is old if

_____

_____

All shoes _____

_____

Some shoes _____

_____

3. Describe the shoes you are wearing today. Include as much detail as you can.

_____

_____

_____

_____

_____

_____

4. Here are the shoe tracks of two people walking in the snow. Be a good detective and tell us anything you can about the people who made the tracks.

_____

_____

_____

The Fast Page

Possible Responses:

1. In the time it takes to count to ten, she could run all the way around the world. She ran so quickly that the wind would blow you down when she zoomed past.

2. The second one. The letters are leaning, like people do when they are running fast.

3. You wouldn't know when the word "go" was going to be said, so you'd never be ready.

4. When I go to the carnival, I have so much fun it seems like the time just flies by.

5.

Comment:

Share some of the tall tales from Number 1 with the class.

Extender:

Take the opportunity here to introduce fast drawing. Have a member of the class come up to the front of the room and do some 10-second action poses. Instruct the rest of the class to try to draw the poses quickly. The end results should look something like the examples shown below.

Name_____

THE ___ FAST PAGE

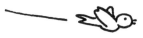

1. Hurry! Write a tall tale about the world's fastest person. What's a tall tale? It's a story that no one could possibly believe. One rule: You have to work with the words that are already there.

In the time it takes to count to ten, she _____

_____

_____ so quickly that _____

_____

_____

2. Circle the word that looks faster. Explain your choice.

FAST   *FAST*

_____

_____

_____

_____

4. Write about something that always seems to get over with too fast.

_____

_____

_____

3. "ON YOUR MARK, GET SET, GO!"

Why don't they just say "Go!" to start a race?

_____

_____

_____

5. What is your favorite fast-food restaurant? What do you usually order?

_____

_____

_____

75

The Furniture Page

Possible Responses:

1. Furniture is usually thought of as large, moveable objects which are used in a home or office.

2.

3. A drawer is like a box with no lid that slides in and out of a piece of furniture, like a chest or a desk. It holds things, and helps to keep them clean and out of sight.

4. If an "h" can look like a chair, then two "T's" can look like a table.

   If an "o," an "l," and a "c" can look like a lamp, then an "E," an "l," and two "o's" can look like a chest.

Comment:

Number 1 is tough. Children will probably define furniture as "things like tables and chairs and couches." That's good enough.

Extender:

In the spirit of Number 4, instruct students to draw a living room that features "alphabet" furniture, and have them even put some "alphabet" people in the room. It'll be interesting to see how youngsters handle the challenge.

Name_____

THE  FURNITURE PAGE ~

I wish I had a sofa!

1. A sink is not furniture, but a table is. What is furniture really?

_____

_____

2. Describe one piece of furniture in your living room. Put in lots of details. What is it? Where is it? What is its color? What is it made of?

_____

_____

_____

3. What is a drawer? How does it work? What is it used for?

_____

_____

_____

4. Look at these drawings and finish the sentences in a logical way.

   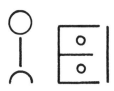

If an "h" can look like a chair, then two "T's" can . . .

If an "o," an "l," and a "c" can look like a lamp, then . . .

_____   _____

_____   _____

_____   _____

The My Page

Possible Responses:

1. My first tooth came out when I was five and it hurt a lot when my dad helped me pull it.

   My favorite food is tacos because I like food that is hot, and I really like salsa.

   My only pet is my dog and her name is Susie, and I was the one to give her that name.

2.

3. My, oh my!
   There's a
   spoon
   in the sky.

   My, oh my!
   There's a
   candle
   on the pie.

   My, oh my!
   There's an
   apple with
   an eye.

Comment:

Some students will have a hard time shifting gears for the apple-eye rhyme in Number 3. Don't offer assistance. Just tell them "my, oh my, give it another try."

Extender:

Have students illustrate one of the sentences they wrote for Number 1.

THE MY PAGE ~

1. Help! These "my" sentences need endings. But here's one rule: Each of your sentences must fill up both of the lines.

My first _____

_____

My favorite _____

_____

My only _____

_____

2. Here is an exact description of MY last Halloween costume:

_____

_____

_____

_____

_____

_____

3. Be a silly poet! Look at the pictures, then finish the poems by making them rhyme with "my, oh my" in some way.

My, oh my!
There's a

_____

_____

My, oh my!
There's a

_____

_____

My, oh my!
There's an

_____

The Crowded Page

Possible Responses:

1.

2. By the time I got to the parade there were so many people that it was hard to see.

   People were packed so tightly in the elevator that I could not get on.

   You do not call a swarm of bees a crowd and you do not call a herd of cows a flock.

3. They are all smiling and they are all looking in the same direction.

4. The roar (or noise)
   of the crowd
   was really
   quite loud.

Comment:

You might want to continue this "crowded business" by inviting students to write you a "crowded note" in their spare time.

Extender:

Challenge youngsters to draw a picture of a crowd of stick figures hanging, climbing, and scrambling all over a jungle gym.

Name_____

 THE CROWDED PAGE

 Hey! You spelled "crow."

1. Think of the biggest crowd you have ever been in. Write as much as you can about the experience. What was going on? Who else was there? How did you feel?

_____

_____

_____

_____

_____

2. CROWDED
   SENTENCES

Finish these crowded sentences. You will
need to crowd your answers, too.

BythetimeIgottotheparadethereweresomanypeoplethat _____

Peoplewerepackedsotightlyintheelevatorthat _____

Youdonotcallaswarmofbeesacrowdandyoudonotcallaherd _____

3. Write two things you notice about this crowd of people.

_____

_____

_____

4. FINISH THE POEM.

The _____

of the crowd

was really

quite _____.

The Bug Page

Possible Responses:

1. All bugs have six legs.
   Grasshoppers are tremendous jumpers.
   Beetles never burp or buy bananas.

2. Bugs are everywhere.

   I really like little ladybugs.

   Bugs come in many different shapes and forms, and some are nice but some are not so nice!

3. A bug smelled cake that two people were eating at a picnic table. It buzzed down for a bite and almost got swatted. As it flew away it said, in tiny bug talk, "Thanks for the dessert."

Comment:

You might want to extend the first activity by introducing some other instructions, such as "Write a sentence about bugs that ends very abruptly." Or "Write a sentence about bugs that seems to flow smoothly." Or "Write a sentence about bugs that has too many adjectives."

Extender:

Have students draw some imaginary bugs they wouldn't want to see.

Name_____

THE BUG PAGE

1. Don't let this assignment "bug" you. Follow the directions carefully.

Write a sentence about bugs that has correct facts but is not very interesting.

_____

Write a sentence about bugs that uses some big words.

_____

Write a sentence about bugs that uses as many "B" words as possible.

_____

2. BUGS

Write a three-word sentence about bugs.

_____

Write a five-word sentence about bugs.

_____

_____

Now, using as many words as you wish, write a long sentence about bugs.

_____

_____

_____

_____

3. A BUG STORY

Look at the pictures, and write a little story about what could be happening to this bug.

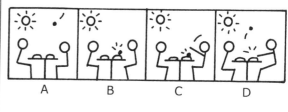

A   B   C   D

_____

_____

_____

_____

_____

_____

The Next Page

Possible Responses:

1.

2. Yellow sunflowers in the garden are so tall, they seem to reach up to the sky.

3. First, get out a piece of bread. Then, put the bread in the toaster. Next, put the toast down and wait for it to pop up.

   First, wet your hair. Then, put shampoo on it. Now, rinse it. Next, dry it. Finally, comb it.

4. A mouse next to a house next to a ring next to a king next to a spoon next to a moon next to a hat next to a bat.

Comment:

Congratulations, you have a class of poets, if students have read the pictures in Number 4 correctly.

Extender:

Ask students to illustrate the sentence they wrote for Number 2.

Name_____

THE N→E→X→T PAGE

I'm next!

1. Who is one of your next-door neighbors? Describe that person as well as you can. Include some interesting details.

_____

_____

_____

_____

2. Write a long sentence about flowers. It must start with the next-to-the-last letter in the alphabet.

_____

_____

3. Finish these sentences in a way that makes sense.

First, get out a piece of bread. Then, put the bread in the toaster.

Next, _____

_____

First, wet your hair. Then, _____

Now, rinse it. Next, _____ Finally, comb it.

4. Look at the pictures and continue the pattern.

A mouse next to a house next _____

_____

_____

The Air Page

Possible Responses:

1. We don't know what we'll do.
    He doesn't think about what he's doing.
    She missed the basket, the backboard, and everything.

2. My hand felt cooler after I blew on it.
    My breath made my hand feel warmer.

3. A giant loaf of bread just flew by my head! I had to duck down or it might have hit me. It looked like someone had just taken a big bite out of it, and the bread seemed to be really mad. Did I tell you how big it was? It was as big as a car!

Comment:

Responses to Number 3 should give you some insight into the imaginative prowess of various students.

Extender:

Use this opportunity to have students draw a picture about a day when the air is moving fast – in other words, a windy day.

THE AIR PAGE

I'd better stay out of the way!

1. Even if you don't know for sure, write what you think these three "airy" sayings might mean.

Our plans are still up in the air. _____

_____

He is a real airhead. _____

_____

The basketball player shot an air ball. _____

_____

2. AIR EXPERIMENTS

Lick the back of your hand and then blow on it. Write a sentence about what you notice.

_____

_____

_____

Take a deep breath and let it out slowly with your hand close to your nose and mouth. Write a sentence about what you notice.

_____

_____

3. Write a tall tale no one will believe about something you have just seen up in the air. Let your imagination go wild, and include many details!

_____

_____

_____

_____

_____

_____

_____

_____

The Boring Page

Possible Responses:

1. Something is usually boring when it's the same all the time, or when it's something you do over and over.

2. A television set is a big black box. When it is turned on, it shows pictures.

3. Design B is the most boring. The lines are all the same length, and they are arranged in a regular-looking pattern.

4. I think the job of working in a factory would be boring. You would do the same thing over and over.

5. I think being an artist would not be boring. You would get to use many of your own ideas. And every time you started to work, you wouldn't know what to expect.

Comment:

Take a cue from Number 2 and have students do oral descriptions of classroom items in the most boring way they can. Then, if there is time, do the opposite: exciting descriptions.

Extender:

Have children draw a very boring-looking person wearing boring-looking clothes standing next to an exciting-looking person wearing exciting-looking clothes.

Name_____

Snore yawn ²² dull z ho-hum

THE BORING PAGE

Birds are never bored.

1. What makes something boring? Try to explain. _____

_____

_____

_____

2. Describe a television set in the most boring way you can. _____

_____

_____

_____

3. Which of these designs do you think is the most boring? Explain your answer.

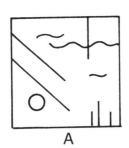   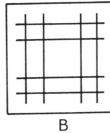   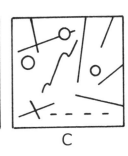

A   B   C

_____

_____

_____

4. Name a job you think might be boring and tell why. _____

_____

_____

5. Name a job you think would <u>not</u> be boring and tell why. _____

_____

_____

89

The Mistake Page

Possible Responses:

1. It was a great day. The sun was out and it made me feel happy.

2. kitchen: I could burn toast or spill something or forget to cook the vegetables or cut my finger.

   school: I could give some wrong answers on a test or whisper when I shouldn't or not get back from lunch on time.

   store: I could forget my money or buy a shirt in the wrong size or bump into something and knock it over.

3.

4. I made
   a mistake
   when I
   baked
   the cake.

Comment:

Number 2 encourages children to generate a number of ideas about each situation, thus promoting fluency.

Extender:

Have students draw a picture of a house, putting in as many mistakes as they can. (A door on the second floor, crooked windows, an upside-down house number, and so forth.)

THE MISTAKE PAGE

Name_____

I'm a brid!

1. *OOPs!* Someone crossed out some mistakes. Write this paragraph again, filling in your own words where the mistakes have been made.

It was a ~~xxxx~~ day. The ~~xxxx~~ was ~~xxxx~~ and it made me feel ~~xxxx~~

_____

_____

_____

2. What are some mistakes you could make if you were in these places?

kitchen _____

_____

school _____

_____

store _____

_____

3. MISTAKEN IDEAS 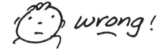 *wrong!*

When you were smaller, did you ever have the wrong idea about something? Write about it.

I used to think that _____

_____

_____

_____

4. FINISH THE POEM.

I _____

a mistake

when I

_____

_____

The Fact Page

Possible Responses:

1.

2. Fireflies come out on summer nights.
   Apples grow on trees.
   Cows have four legs.
   Taxis take people places.

3. I could throw a ball up, and watch it come down.
   I could look in the telephone directory.

Comment:

If you have time, you might want to read a variety of statements, some of which are facts and some of which are opinions, and have a class discussion about the differences between the two.

Extender:

Ask students to illustrate at least one of their facts in Number 2.

THE (FACT) PAGE

I'm about
3 inches tall.

1. Facts are things you know for sure. Write a short paragraph that contains several facts about our classroom.

_____

_____

_____

_____

_____

2. Write four facts about things that start with the letters below. For example, you could say "Fish have gills," and "Airplanes have wings and tails," but don't use these ideas. Think of some of your own facts!

F _____

A _____

C _____

T _____

3. Here are two facts. Write a sentence about how you could prove them.

FACT 1	FACT 2
A ball is affected by gravity.	Many people in our area are named "Smith."
_____	_____
_____	_____
_____	_____

93

The Worry Page

Possible Responses:

1.

2. A flower might worry about getting picked or not having enough water.

   A loaf of bread might worry about getting sliced or getting eaten.

   A rug might worry about getting walked on or being put in the washing machine.

   A snowman might worry about melting in the hot sun or someone knocking his head off.

3. student – grades
   baby – getting fed
   cook – burning food
   beauty queen – make-up
   teacher – grading tests
   politician – votes

Comment:

About Number 1: We have deliberately avoided asking children what worries them now, since many youngsters wouldn't necessarily want to share this information. But asking them about something that worried them when they were little is fair game.

Extender:

Ask students to draw a picture of themselves (or you, if you're a risk-taker) looking very, very worried.

Cats, Hawks...

1. Write about something that worried you when you were little.

_____

_____

_____

_____

_____

_____

2. If these things could worry, what are <u>two</u> things each of them might worry about?

A flower might worry about _____

_____

_____

A loaf of bread might worry about _____

_____

_____

A rug might worry about _____

_____

_____

A snowman might worry about _____

_____

3. What might these people worry about?

student

_____

baby

_____

cook

_____

beauty queen

_____

teacher

_____

politician

_____

The Pointy Page

Possible Responses:

1. A nail is a long, thin piece of metal with a head and a sharp point.

2. The pencil point broke so I had to sharpen it.
   If my team had scored just one more point, we would have won.
   When the clock hands point straight up, it's midnight or noon.

3. Two birds are having a fight and pecking at each other.

4. If bugs had arms they might hold things.
   I have a lot of icky bugs crawling on my arms.

Comment:

There are many ways Number 3 can be interpreted. In addition to bird beaks, the points could be two ice cream cones that have fallen on the ground, two clown hats resting on a table, some very sharp elbows, two people dueling with swords, etc.

Extender:

Have students make a big bird out of pointy shapes – pointy feathers, a pointy beak, pointy claws, perhaps a pointy tuft on top of the head.

I'm pointing!

1. Describe a nail using just one sentence.

_____

_____

_____

2. Use the word "point" in a sentence about a pencil, a sentence about a sports team, and a sentence about a clock.

_____

_____

_____

_____

_____

_____

_____

_____

3. Think of something this could be and write about it.

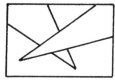

_____

_____

_____

_____

4. The arrows are pointing at just two words. Figure out what the words are and then write two sentences that contain both words.

also giraffes shelf soda bugs
sunshine arms water moo
salad many money green desk
and

_____

_____

_____

_____

The On and Off Page

Possible Responses:

1. I put a bandage on my knee.
   There are four wheels on every car.
   I took off my coat because it was a warm day.
   I had to turn on the light so that I could see.

2. A. The wind blew the boy's hat off and it landed on the dog.
   B. Somebody marked on the wall, so my mom had to wipe it off.
   C. The airplane took off on a very rainy day.

3. Keep your   I turned the TV on
   freezer on   but the program
   or your ice will soon   made me
   be gone.   yawn.

Comment:

We have placed "bandage-knee" first in Number 1 because it is the easiest and should help students get off on the right foot.

Extender:

Have students draw a picture that expresses this: A bird on a hat on a clown on a chair on a table.

Name_____

THE ON and OFF PAGE

I'm on a branch!

1. Write four sentences, using the words you see. Each sentence must also include one of these two words: "on" or "off."

(bandage – knee) _____

_____

(four – car) _____

_____

(took – day) _____

_____

(turn – see) _____

_____

2. Describe each of these pictures with a sentence which includes the words "on" and "off."

 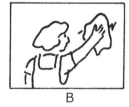 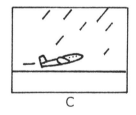

A   B   C

A. _____

_____

B. _____

_____

C. _____

_____

3. "ON" POEMS

Finish these "on" poems with words that rhyme.

Keep your freezer on or your ice will soon

be _____

I turned the TV on but the program made me

_____

The Candy Page

Possible Responses:

1. Milky Way.

   It has a brown, green and white paper wrapper, and there's some writing on the side or bottom of the wrapper.

   It's shaped like a rectangle and all you can see is creamy milk chocolate on the outside.

   The very first bite is the most delicious. First, you bite through a chocolate layer to get to a creamy light-brown center layered with rich caramel. There aren't any nuts. I try to take small bites to make it last a long time, but it's hard to do that. The caramel lasts a little bit longer in my mouth than the rest of it. It is so sweet and nice.

2.

Comment:

If you have students who don't eat candy for dietary or other reasons, simply have them describe the merits of raisins, oatmeal cookies, etc.

Extender:

Stretch the candy page a bit to include other sweets. Have children draw pictures of as many sweet things as they can think of. See who can amass the greatest number of sweet images.

Name_____

THE  PAGE

No thanks!

1. What is the name of your favorite candy? _____

Describe its wrapper. _____

_____

What does the outside of the candy look like before you start to eat it?

_____

_____

Now, write about the experience of eating it. How does it feel in your mouth? How does it taste? Is it sweet or sour? Does it have caramel or nuts inside? How long does it take to eat it? Do you try to make it last a long time or do you eat it fast? Do you always eat it the same way? Details, please!

_____

_____

_____

_____

2. Pretend you are a parent and your child has just eaten some candy you said not to eat. How would you handle it? What would you say?

_____

_____

_____

_____

The Tiny Page

Possible Responses:

1. I like to sneak up on my little brother.

2. This is the city where we live with everyone shooting off fireworks on the Fourth of July.

3. The fat bug bit me on the arm. My dog and cat can see me. I sat on wet goo. The toy is in the car.

4. I have a very tiny mouth.
   I have very tiny eyes.
   I have a very tiny nose.

Comment:

The answer for Number 2 can be practically anything, but it must be faithful to the spirit of the introduction. In other words, a student can't get away with an answer such as "a little bug." It should be fun to read some of the responses. In fact, you could have a contest to see who can come up with the zaniest interpretation.

Extender:

Have students fold a piece of paper in half. On the left side, tell them to draw a great big bird in a very tiny cage. On the right side, have them draw a very tiny bird in a very large cage.

THE  PAGE ～

Tiny bird

1. Finish this sentence with words that get smaller and smaller.

I like to

2. If you had a very powerful magnifying glass, you would see that this dot is really a picture of a football stadium with 50,000 people watching a game.

Now, what could this be? →

_____

_____

_____

_____

4. Look at the drawings and finish the sentences. Use the word "tiny" in every sentence.

I have _____

_____

I have _____

_____

I have _____

3. Write several sentences using as many of these tiny words as you can. You can use only the words below, but you can use them more than one time.

I	dog	goo	in	can
bug	bed	and	toy	arm
is	bit	me	sat	wet
the	on	a	my	see
fat	to	cat	ran	car

_____

_____

_____

_____

_____

_____

_____

_____

_____

_____

The Square Page

Possible Responses:

1. A square with a tear. A square with hair. A square on a chair. A bear in a square. A square in the air. A square over there.

2. I see a small square in the middle of a bigger square.
   I see four little squares forming a big square.
   I see four little dark squares in the corners of a big square.

3. I love milk. Or: A book fell. I hate bugs. I fell down. Etc.
   He has four cats. Or: It was very cold. My hat felt warm. Etc.
   I did very poorly. Or: I saw them coming. Etc.

Comment:

Of course, some students are going to have a frustrating time with Number 3, while others will love the challenge. For the students who have trouble, you may have to do a little diplomatic coaching.

Extender:

Have children write you a note using squarish letters. Then you can write a comment back to them in the same manner.

Name_____

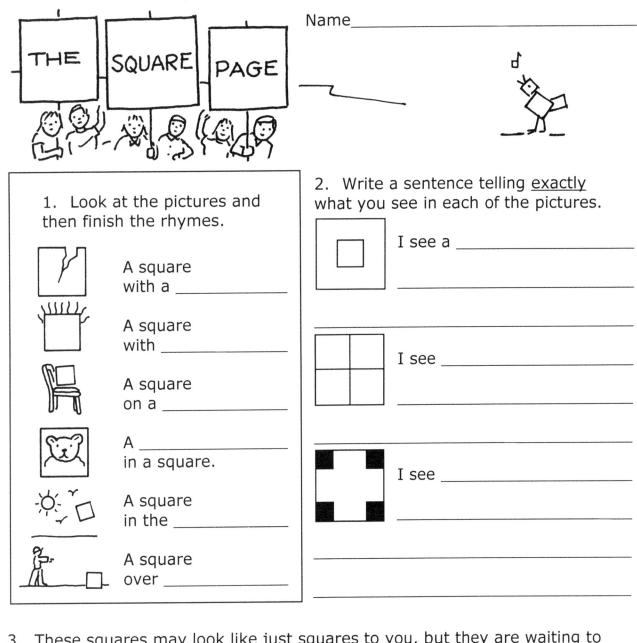

THE SQUARE PAGE

1. Look at the pictures and then finish the rhymes.

A square with a _____

A square with _____

A square on a _____

A _____ in a square.

A square in the _____

A square over _____

2. Write a sentence telling <u>exactly</u> what you see in each of the pictures.

I see a _____
_____

I see _____
_____

I see _____
_____
_____

3. These squares may look like just squares to you, but they are waiting to hold letters that form words and sentences. It's your job to make three sentences. Look at the example and you'll get the idea.

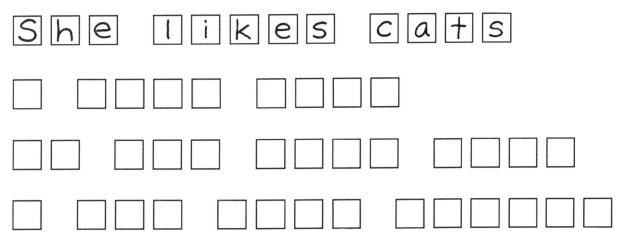

She likes cats

The Vegetable Page

Possible Responses:

1. A carrot is a vegetable that grows in the ground. The main part of it is orange. It looks like a long, skinny, pointy triangle. When it is growing in the ground, it has a green top that sticks up above the ground. You eat the orange part. It is pretty hard, so you have to chew well before you swallow.

2. Our dinner table is round, and we have had it for a long time.

3. I think corn on the cob is the greatest. It has a sweet flavor and is especially good when butter is smeared on it. I like to put a little bit of salt on it, too.

4. Do you carrot all for me?
   I can beet you at tennis.
   Peas, pass the rolls.
   I have bean to the store.

Comment:

About Number 1: This is an activity that can be dashed off in 30 seconds or it can take much longer. Encourage children to dig in and describe all aspects of a carrot. The more details the better.

Extender:

Give children a paper plate and let them "draw" a meal on it. Be sure they include at least one vegetable!

Name_____

THE VEGETABLE PAGE

I prefer seeds!

1. Your friend, Xoglo, from the Planet Alpha B, has never heard of carrots. Use the space below to tell him as much about carrots as you can.

_____

_____

_____

_____

_____

_____

2. Hidden in the word "vegetable" is a place where you might eat your vegetables. Write an interesting sentence using that word.

_____

_____

_____

3. Write a paragraph about your most favorite vegetable or your least favorite vegetable. One rule: You can't use the word "taste" in your paragraph.

This will squash you!

_____

_____

_____

_____

_____

_____

_____

_____

4. Finish these silly vegetable sentences with one more word.

Do you carrot all for _____

I can beet you at _____

Peas, pass the _____

I have bean to the _____

Index

Publications by Tin Man Press

Is It Friday Already? Learning Centers That Work – 30 weeks of centers in 9 subject areas.

Are They Thinking? – A comprehensive, year-long thinking-skills program.

Loosen Up! – Art activities designed to build confidence.

T is for Think – More than 300 drawings spur thinking excitement.

OPQ – Offbeat Adventures With the Alphabet – Center approach based on the alphabet.

Waiting for Lunch – Sponge activities for those little moments in the day.

Great Unbored Bulletin Board Books I and II – 20 great board ideas in each book.

Great Unbored Blackboard Book – Quick analytical activities you do on the board.

WakerUppers – 50 friendly hand-drawn reproducible sheets to motivate thinking.

Nifty Fifty – 500 provocative questions about 50 everyday things.

Smart Snips – Each of the 50 reproducible activities starts with something to cut.

Ideas To Go – 50 different assignments cover a broad range of thinking skills.

Brain Stations – 50 easy-to-make centers promote creative and flexible thinking.

Play by the Rules – 50 scripted challenges turn students into better listeners.

Going Places – Students participate in five interesting listening adventures.

Letter Getters – Letter clues encourage language development and deductive thinking.

Just Write! – 50 motivational thinking and writing activities.

The Discover! Series – 24 card sets provide hands-on experiences with everyday objects.

Adventures of a Dot Series – 10 card sets use a Dot character to encourage thinking.

Linework – Jumbo card set centers around the concept of line.

An Alphabet You've Never Met – Jumbo card set plays creatively with letters.

Phone/Fax: 1-800-676-0459   **Website**: www.tinmanpress.com